THE PSY
OF
PERSUASION

The Secret Psychology of Subconscious Influence

Discovering Success With
One Life Changing Sentence

© 2017 William D. Horton, Psy. D.

NFNLP 1532 US 41 By-Pass. S., #287, Venice, FL 34293

(941) 408-8551 Fax: (941) 408-8552

Email: nfnlp@aol.com Website: www.nfnlp.com

Table of Contents

Preface

With this book, you will be learning techniques to guide a person's actions to do what you want.

Intrigued?

To be fair, this book is NOT about "mind control," because that doesn't exist...well, unless you're a Jedi.

No, this book is about the art of influence. It's an art, in that to become proficient at these techniques, the reader must practice them and deeply understand them. That being said, despite the artfulness of what you're about learn, Dr. Horton provides an amazing amount of science behind this stuff, giving you the background, the history, the why...

In short, you're going to learn how to unlock how a person thinks...it may not be mind-reading (knowing their exact thoughts) but by understanding HOW a person thinks, what motivates them, what do they most hold dear, what keeps them up at night...you'll have the secrets to unlock what drives their behavior.

And understanding those things will enable you to persuade their behavior.

I know this is all true because Dr. Horton has changed my life. I first started learning this amazing technology almost 15 years ago, and while I've learned a lot, by directly working with Dr. Horton in live training as well through his books and other distance learning tools, I can say that the person who approaches this art with the attitude of continued learning, with the idea that mastering such a powerful craft is not going to happen overnight, but as a first step into a larger world (to paraphrase Jedi Master, Obi Wan Kenobi) is going to be the person who gets the most out of this.

In other words, if you're reading this book hoping to score your next one-night stand after reading a few pages of this book, don't bother.

The best way that I can think of to help you, dear reader, understand the journey you're about to go on is with a story...

When I was a little boy, around ten years of age or so, I read a marvelous book called "Runaway Robot." It was a science fiction book, written, it felt, specifically for boys my age with a great imagination. It told the story of a future where mankind (well, humankind to be PC, but the book was written in the 60's) had colonized the moon, Mars, and other places in space.

Families lived on the moon, and occasionally a job change would move a family to Mars, for instance, or perhaps back to Earth. In a way, it was like military families being stationed in different places, but moving the furniture was done with rockets instead of U-Hauls!

One particular family moved back to Earth but in the process, the family robot got left behind. The robot's role for most of these families was to watch over the children, keep them safe, etc. So the robot in this story got left behind and set out to find his family. Think of it as "Home Alone 4: Adventure In Space."

At one point during the robot's various adventures in his quest, his eye bulbs burnt out (Again, it was written in the 60's - nowadays the robot's eyes would probably be plasma powered or some such thing). At any rate, now the robot was blind. As he stumbled along his way, he eventually encountered a wise mechanic, a guru to the robots, if you will.

This wise man helped the robot, nurtured him, and replaced his eye bulbs. As the robot's visual system came back online, the robot regained his sight...but was amazed by what he saw, though he couldn't explain or even comprehend why he was amazed.

"Everything's different!" the robot blurted out.

With a gentle smile, the wise guru said, "That's the COLOR you're seeing."

You see, dear reader, the robot's previous eye bulbs were of a cheaper variety that only allowed the robot to see things in black and white. The newer bulbs were color...so the guru's gift enabled the robot to see so much more in the world that he did not realize was there all along.

Learning the skills in this book will enable you, dear reader, to understand people in ways you could not have imagined...to see the true 'color,' the true inner details in everyone around you...even though it's always been there.

Come to think of it, maybe you WILL become a Jedi along the way.

Enjoy the journey.

- Cris Johnson

Board Certified Hypnotist and Certified Trainer of Hypnosis and Neuro-Linguistic Programming

Most people avoid studying the topic of persuasion in depth. This can be due to ignorance, a lack of interest, or even fear. They don't know that even the most basic tools of persuasion can transform their lives. Persuasion can seem to be a sophisticated technique to grasp, considering the complicated minds of human beings. But upon further study, we can begin to blow away the smoke that surrounds this skill that is essential to our success.

Persuasion can't be defined by thousands of laws, and it cannot be wrestled down into a textbook either. Not effectively, at least. Unlike math or science, persuasion is not considered to be a universal language.

Persuasion may be the best tool in existence for dealing with people, so investing in the skills outlined here could end up being imperative to your future success.

You can learn the universal truth, the *one sentence* that covers all areas of persuasion and applies it wholly or in part throughout your life, to achieve the results that you desire.

With this sentence, you'll rise above the world's population. You will find that what you want to happen, can happen more often than not.

Simplicity is often very powerful. Think of the varieties of beverage from which to choose. With such variety, why do we crave water when we are overly thirsty? It is because the simple satisfies our basic needs without overstimulating our senses.

Everybody instinctively wants to be better at persuasion, whether they consciously know this or not. It isn't like basketball or painting, where the interest is subjective. Persuasion is highly valued because it is a tool to exhort your will onto the world. Again, *persuasion is a tool to exhort your will onto the world.*

First, it is important to define persuasion and reveal why it methods of persuasion are necessary.

Your Will and Persuasion

Human beings will always have desires. Growing up means learning that sometimes we just can't get what we want. It's a hard lesson, and most people still have not come to full terms with it. Life is a constant conflict between the ideal vision we have in our minds while trying to achieve this same vision in reality. Our mind loves the linear, to go from A to B. We dream up plans and ideas for our futures, but life often has an entirely different plan for us.

Some people have solved this issue by choosing to see what they want to see. They live to wallow in their ignorance. Instead of forcing their will onto the world, they pretend and live as far away from reality as they can. They unconsciously project themselves onto other people, unable to understand other points of view or make an effort to care about them. Routines and quotas are bread and butter for these people. Anything with a bit more 'spice' is too daunting to comprehend. These individuals will never grasp the message of this book.

Some other people are ruled by negativity. They see that they have little control over the world and this affects them. They become depressed when things don't go their way. They are always anxious and regret the failings of the past. They can only sit back and watch, as life deals their cards *and* plays the game for them. As the eternal spectators, these people could learn a lot from this book by taking a leap of faith.

There are also those that recognize the truth. These people know that you can't control everything in life. They experience failures like everyone else, but there is an essential difference in the process.

These people are not passive. These people know that there are significant parts of life that fall under their control, for which they are wholly responsible. Alternately, they understand that there are also things in life that they simply will never be able to control. They know that they aren't able to fly or move objects with their mind, but understand how to use their skills effectively. Persuasion is one of these skills.

Simply put, persuasion means the ability to influence others to do your bidding.

Babies cry when they are hungry, and toddlers throw tantrums when they hear something that they do not like. Adults often use the same juvenile methods to get what they want out of people, but few experience successes with these methods.

These methods are primitive. Becoming frustrated, angry, anxious, depressed, or rude toward others is a choice that will never help any adult to achieve success. People have a tolerance for children, but it is a different set of rules when you are among adults. No matter what you are asking of someone, they likely will not do it if you are yelling at them.

As adults, it is important to develop techniques to make sure that your interests are heard. Ensure that people respect what you need, and are willing to give it to you. Most people settle for just being polite, for mediocre skills of persuasion. Those who know the real value of persuasion, however, treat it as an art form and study it like the gospel.

Persuasion isn't just for people who care only about making a commission. Everyone has their self-interest, their life, and they have to navigate it as best they can. It isn't morally wrong to want to be able to ask for a raise or to convince your spouse to watch the movie you want to watch, or even to barter with your child so that they will clean their room without complaint.

If you want to be able to get what you want, then this book was written with you in mind. Persuasion can make your inner world a reality.

HUMAN HARDWARE

Throughout history a perplexing question of mankind has been "why are some people more successful than others?" While the complex explanation involves the interplay between genes, physical environment, socioeconomic and cultural indicators, the simple explanation involves **programming.**

In the early 1970s, a team of scientists at the University of California at Santa Cruz set out to answer the question of why people with similar backgrounds of education, training, and experience were not similarly successful. They wanted to explore what they called "the secrets of effective people" and wanted to "model human excellence". What they discovered between people is that, while backgrounds were similar, the brain wiring – or programming -- was distinctly different. What developed out of this research was the field of neurolinguistics programming. The word "neurolinguistics" is actually a combination of three words:

- neuro: referring to the brain
- linguistic: referring to content (verbal and non-verbal)
- programming: manipulation of content

Neurolinguistics programming rests on the premise that thought patterns (programming) are largely responsible for an individual's success or failure; that preconceived thoughts and mental conditioning effect our social interactions and accomplishments. The theory is that if you remodel your negative thoughts, you can change your personal situation. This "remodeling" of thoughts requires a process called neurogenesis.

Neurogenesis

Simply described, neurogenesis is the creation of new nerve connections in the brain. These nerve connections are somewhat similar to the hardwiring of a computer. While the computer relies on hardware composed of digital circuitry, the human brain relies on hardware composed of neural circuitry – composed of billions of neurons (nerve cells) forming a complex neurological system (nervous system). These neurons assess the human environment and react accordingly by sending chemical messages to each other through electrical impulses. These messages form the basis of our learning, productivity, behavior, and very survival.

Neurogenesis is essential to success in humans. As we often look to scientific studies of other species to explain processes in humans, let me share a fascinating study of canaries. Frederick Nottebohm's studies performed in the early 1990s illustrate the importance of neurogenesis in songbirds. The songbird depends on its beautiful melodies to attract a mate and produce offspring, ensuring its lineage. In his studies, Nottenbohm discovered that in order to sing these complex melodies, the male birds continually generated new brain cells in their song center. In fact, approximately 1% new neurons are created in the song center daily. Because human behavior is so individually varied, we cannot assess the daily potential of new neural connections, but just compare the canary brain capacity to that of a human and imagine the possibilities!

While you may have heard the statement that humans use only 10% of their brains, this is not exactly true. The correct statement is that humans use only 10% of their neurons at any given time (due to the sheer volume and task specifications). However, this means that the newer neural connections you build the greater productivity you can expect from your active 10%.

The Brain as Computer

We previously compared the brain's neural circuitry to the hardwiring of a computer. Let us further explore this comparison. Both the computer and the human brain have massive information processing ability that is based on the transmission of electrical signals, and both have a memory that can grow and learn to accommodate changing needs. However, both can also become damaged with faulty programming information. For a computer this faulty information comes in the form of viruses; for the human brain it is negativity. Fortunately, both systems can be changed and modified to correct this damage.

However, there is a fundamental difference between computer hardware and the human neurological system. The difference is that while computing hardware may vastly vary from person to person, every person possesses the same neural hardware. There is a common basic physical neurology with billions of neurons processing approximately 40,000 bits of information per second, aiding the brain in reasoning, learning, and memory. In the absence of a disease process, or physical damage or defect, we all possess the same neural hardware. Consider this carefully: ***every human being shares the***

4

same neural hardware. So, if we all share the same hardware, then we all share the same potential!

If we all have the same potential shouldn't we all be equally successful? Again, programming is the underlying answer to why some people are more successful than others. Most of us have heard the old axiom of "it is not what you have but how you use it". In brain neurology, this rings true. The actual wiring of your brain – the number of neural connections -- depends on your individual programming. Too often, mental resources are underutilized and the wiring is subsequently damaged through faulty programming. Chemical abuse can also damage the wiring. Proper programming involves positive nurturing input. Until the last decade, the prevailing scientific theory of neurology was that the human brain could not establish new neural connections. In other words, what you are born with is what you have and as you age they will die. It is now known that the more than one hundred billion neurons of the brain are geared to reinvest in themselves. Positive, enriched environments stimulate the brain to create more neural connections. The more you learn, the more you become capable of learning. You can actually rewire, or reprogram, your brain! You can do this at any age, the more you stimulate it. the more it grows!

Negative Programming

While positive programming stimulates neurogenesis, negative programming halts neurogenesis. Negative programming includes feedback which acts as a stressor. A stressor, whether internal or external, produces a biochemical stress response. Following, we will discuss stressors and the stress response process.

The stress response process was first described by Hans Selye in the 1930s as "the rate of wear and tear on the body". Broadly, the term describes the biochemical reaction to a threat to biological balance (also known as homeostasis). While researchers agree on the physiological and psychological effects of stress on the human body, the term itself remains somewhat of an abstract concept because it is dependent on human perception. In other words, the occurrence of stressors as well as the degree of stress response depends on individual situational analysis. This means that it is not set in stone and it can be altered!

5

Stressors can be either external (coming from someone else) or internal (coming from yourself). Stressors fall into categories of

- positive (eustress) or negative (distress)
- acute or chronic
- mental or physical

From these categories, many combinations can occur, and not all are bad. Acute stress is actually helpful, temporarily flooding the body with hormones to assist in regaining homeostasis. For example, positive-acute-mental stress could be exemplified by the exuberation of winning a Nobel Prize. Certainly no one could call this a bad thing, but the body still gets a little overwhelmed and needs to regain balance! Alternatively, chronic stress is damaging, continually flooding the body with hormones, which over time can damage mental functions. As an example, negative-chronic-mental stress could come in the form of everyday worries such as low self-esteem. Low self-esteem is an example of negative programming. It also becomes self-reinforcing.

Regardless of the source, the effect of continued stress from negative programming is neurologically toxic. What this means is that when the brain is constantly exposed to worry and negativity, homeostasis (balance) becomes the priority and all other neural functioning suffers. In this situation, existing neurons are preoccupied with survival and the brain does not exert effort on creating new neurons.

Again looking to another species to explain human processes, Elizabeth Gould's studies have documented this chronic stress effect in primates. These studies show that when a primate is under chronic stress "its brain begins to starve. It stops creating new cells. The cells it already has retreat inwards. The mind is disfigured."

Broken Windows Theory

"Broken Windows" is a social theory relating to urban vandalism. The theory states that if windows are broken and left unrepaired in an abandoned building, the community will believe that this vandalism is acceptable. Further, if left unaddressed, the vandalism will spread into other parts of the community. However, immediate repair of the broken windows and steps to prevent future incident sends the message that vandalism is not acceptable and will not be tolerated.

The same theory has been expanded to graffiti, thus the push to "clean up the environment".

This same theory could be applied to negative programming of the human brain. If the brain is exposed to negative programming without intervention, the individual will believe that this is acceptable. The same can be applied to failure, if accepted, it becomes the norm. If left unaddressed, this will develop into chronic mental stress, affecting the structure of the brain and reducing the success potential of the individual. However, introduction of positive programming will rewire the brain, producing new neural connections and increasing individual success potential.

CALIBRATION SKILLS

The way we speak grows out of the mental or thinking processes in our brain. In order to function, these mental processes need the help of certain bodily and physiological processes for consolidation and expression. These physical reactions are important. They give observers an opportunity to understand and confirm what kind of mental processes are going on with the speaker. By paying close attention to specific behaviors as others communicate, we can know the structure of their thoughts. We cannot tell what they are thinking, but we can know "how" **they are thinking**. Once we know this we can lead them into the change work that they want.

A. People primarily represent themselves in one of three categories:
1. Visuals (sight).
2. Auditories (hearing).
3. Kinesthetic (feeling).

B. Visuals:
1. A good example of a strong Visual is "Robin Williams." Visuals comprise approximately **60%** of the population in the United States.

2. Speech Pattern:
a. Fast.
b. Broken Sentences.
c. Staccato.

3. Gestures:
a. In front, where they can see them.
b. They use their hands a lot.

4. Language:
>> **a.** Visual Terms "I <u>see</u> what you are saying." "I get the picture."

5. Eye Movement:
>> **a.** Up and to the left for something remembered.
>> **b.** Up and to the right for something conceptualized.

6. Breathing:
>> **a.** Shallow ... upper half of the chest.
>> **b.** Often appear out of breath when they talk.

7. Dress:
>> **a.** Matched.
>> **b.** Colorful.
>> **c.** Very mindful of how they look.
>> **d.** Jewelry.

8. Thought Process:
>> **a.** Very fast.
>> **b.** Make pictures.
>> **c.** Speed of light versus the speed of sound.
>> **d.** They see the world primarily through pictures.

9. Miscellaneous:
>> **a.** They comprise approximately 60% of the population.
>> **b.** Movers and shakers.
>> **c.** Very precise in what they want. Short ... brief ... to the point.
>> **d.** They like graphs, charts.
>> **e.** Would rather live in a city where there is action and lights (eye candy) than in the country.
>> **f.** Socialites at parties, moving around talking to everyone.

C. Auditories:

A good example is "Former President Reagan." They comprise approximately 25% of the population in the United States.

1. Speech:
>> **a.** Slow, rhythmic.
>> **b.** Conversational, purposeful.

2. Gestures:
    a. To the side toward the ears.
    b. Tug on their ear a lot.

3. Language Pattern:
    a. Very auditory *"I hear what you are saying." "That is clear as a bell."*
    b. They like to talk to themselves (especially digital auditories).
    c. Often speak in dialogue.
    d. Some people can be seen "mouthing" words to themselves as they listen and process what another person is saying.

4. Eye movement:
    a. Level, to the left ear for something remembered.
    b. Level, to the right ear for something conceptualized.
    c. Down, and to the left (digital) when they talk to themselves (might even be out loud).

5. Breathing:
    a. Deep, regular, rhythmic, somewhat slower.
    b. Mid chest range.

6. Dress:
    a. More casual.
    b. Still matching.
    c. More muted colors.

7. Thought Process:
    a. Slower, more deliberate.
    b. Think of the speed of sound versus the speed of light.
    c. They have to talk things over with themselves to hear how it sounds.

8. Miscellaneous:
    a. They have a kinship with nature.
    b. Strong auditories love animals as much as people.
    c. Would rather live in the country, than a city (it's quieter).
    d. Hates distracting noises.
    e. Would probably be seen huddled in a corner at a party talking to a select few people.

D. Kinesthetic:

example would be President Clinton or Jimmy Swaggert. They make up about 15% of the population.

1. Speech:
        a. Much slower, more deliberate.
        b. Appears somewhat broken.
        c. Much more feeling.

2. Gestures:
        a. In close.
        b. Touches chest or rubs chin.

3. Language Pattern:
        a. Uses feeling terms *"I'm not sure how I feel about this."*

4. Eye Movement:
        a. One movement, down and to the right.

5. Breathing:
        a. Very deep (belly breathing)
        b. Appears to take very deep breaths.

6. Dress:
        a. Very casual.
        b. Comfort is the name of the game.
        c. Matching is not as important.

7. Thought Process:
        a. Very slow. Methodical.
        b. Has to apply feeling to what he/she is thinking about.

8. Miscellaneous:
        a. Would rather stay home and "cuddle" in front of a fire.
        b. Dislikes crowds and parties.
        c. Likes to get in touch with their feelings.
        d. Moody, either really up or down (not manic / depressive).
        e. Huggy ... likes the feeling of being close to someone.

EYE ACCESSING MOVEMENTS

EYE MOVEMENTS:

Automatic, unconscious eye movements usually accompany a particular thought processes, indicating the accessing of one or more of the sensory representational systems.

When people are thinking and talking they move their eyes in what are known as eye-scanning patterns. These movements appear to be symptomatic of their attempts to gain access to internally stored or internally generated information in their central nervous system. This information is encoded in the speaker's mind in one or more of the representational systems. When a person "goes inside" to retrieve a memory or to create a new thought, the person "makes pictures", and/or "talks to one or more of the representational systems. When a person "goes inside" to retrieve a memory or to create a new thought, the person "makes pictures", and/or "talks to himself/herself", and/or "has feelings and kinesthetic sensations."

With a little bit of practice, eye-scanning patterns are easily observable behavior. When you see people talking and thinking you can notice their eyes are constantly in motion, darting back and forth, up and down, occasionally glancing at objects and people, but just as often "focused"

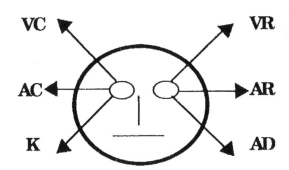

The diagram illustrates the direction of a person's eye accessing movements as you are facing and looking at the person.

When we process information internally, we can do it visually, auditorialy, kinesthetically, olfactorily, or gustatorily. It is possible to access the meaning of a word in any one, or a combination, of the five sensory channels.

Vc   Visual Constructed:
seeing images of things never seen before, or seeing things differently than they were seen before. Questions include: "What will you look like at 90?"

Ac   Auditory Constructed:
hearing sounds not heard before. Questions include: "What would your name sound like backwards?" "How would a dog barking, a car horn and children playing sound like?"

K   Kinesthetic:
feeling emotions, tactile sensations (sense of touch), or proprioceptive feeling (feelings of muscle movement). Questions include: "Is your nose cold now?" "What does it feel like to run?"

Vr   Visual Remembered:
seeing images of things seen before, in the same way they were seen before. Questions include: "What does your coat look like?"

Ar   Auditory Remembered:
remembering sounds heard before. Questions include: "What's the last thing I said?" "What does your alarm clock sound like?"

Ad   Auditory Digital:
talking to oneself. Questions include: "Say something to yourself that you often say." "Recite the pledge of allegiance."

V   Visual:
the blank stare is visual - either constructed or remembered.

A good example of how you can use eye accessing cues is in the case of a car sale, a salesman might stress different features to a customer depending on which is the customer's primary representational system in order to "step into his model of the world." For an **_auditory_** customer, the salesman could stress the thud of the reinforced doors, the upscale stereo system the whisper quiet ride. To a **_visual_** customer, the salesman would stress the clean, sleek lines, the clear view of the scenery through the large tinted windows and sun roof, and ask them to picture themselves behind the wheel, etc. A

kinesthetic person might respond more to the feel of the full grain leather seats, the smooth ride that makes you feel like you are floating on air, feeling of the wind in their hair and the warm sun on their face through the sun roof as they drive along the highway. You also have to stress that even though they have a primary system, you should use appeals to all systems because we all use more than one system. This would also take into account another person who might be involved in the decision process, i.e. the spouse or parent accompanying the buyer, etc.

As a therapist it is easy to understand that it is just another way of gaining rapport with the client and then phrasing your inductions using a representational system to which they are most likely to respond.

In your personal life an **_auditory_** husband might leave socks on the floor, dishes on the table, shoes in the corner, newspapers here and there. A **_visual_** wife might feel that she married a total slob who doesn't appreciate that she tries to create a pleasant tidy house. If he loved me, she thinks, he would care that I spent all day cleaning, etc. On the other hand, the auditory husband may come home from work and sit down to read the paper. Meanwhile, the wife has the food processor running making supper, the TV is on, one teenager is blaring the CD player, and the other one is teasing a barking dog. The husband who is auditory and trying to engage a visual task, screams "Can't I get some peace and quiet in my own home?" Again misunderstandings can occur. It might save a trip to divorce court if both realized:

To this wife, the visual appearance of the home or her clothes, or the lawn is important to her, but makes little impression on an auditory person.

To this husband, the bombardment of all these sounds at once would be like a visual person watching a laser show in an electrical storm.

Just understanding differences can make things run much smoother.

E   Why is this important to you?
    1. You are in the business of communicating with people.

2. Effective communication is critical for all people; it is said we are all sales people as well whatever else we do.
3. When talking to a person in their representational type, rapport is established much more quickly because people like people who are like themselves.
4. Learn how to communicate with people in all three categories. When in Rome....
5. Learning NLP Rapport Building Skills will make you a more effective manager, salesperson, communicator, parent, supervisor, teacher, customer service provider, counselor, lawyer, etc.

By effectively calibrating as to those things we are also able to understand human thinking and behavior. We are able to do this by directing our conscious efforts to seeing, hearing, and sensing the other person's internal representations through the external manifestation of same. If I know that you are making pictures internally (visual), then I can establish deep rapport with you by entering your world using visual language. Or, if I know that you are talking to yourself internally (auditory digital), my rapport-building behavior will involve auditory language. Conversely, if I am aware that your experience is centering on kinesthetic awareness, then my language will be oriented toward touch and feelings. The following information covers five physiological clues that tell you "how" another person is thinking. Not what the person is thinking, but how the person is thinking.

RAPPORT

R eally listen to your client

A ctively follow and model their breathing

P ositively respond to their conversation

P osture – follow, copy, lead

O bserve eye movements

R espond and relate with appropriate V.A.K.

T alk at their speed with their inflections

R eally

A ll

P eople

P refer

O thers

R esembling

T hem

The next process to master is Rapport. This is where you establish trust and credibility. To do this you must first be able to meet people on their terms, not yours, because all people have the idea of "What's in it for me?" running in the background. This is not as difficult as one would think, in fact if we use the rules of waking hypnosis, it is quite simple. What we do is speed up the natural process of friendship.

We all know that a lot, if not most, communication take place in a non-verbal way, so why not use this? How many times have you heard, it not just what you say, it how you say it? If you bear this in mind, as well as the fact you cannot not communicate, let's take this from unconscious to conscious, so we can do this skill at will.

You have been mirroring all of your life. This is how you learned as a child. You learned verbal communication by going through 3 stages, babbling, mirroring, and echolia. You AUTOMATICALLY will mirror anyone you are in rapport with.

Rapport Key: People like others who are like them.

- Have you ever yawned because someone else yawned?
- When a friend stubs their toe, do you flinch that leg or foot and make the same type of face?
- Have you ever looked up because others were looking up?
- Have you ever started itching because you watched some else itch?
- Have you ever picked up a Southern accent, because you were talking to someone from the south?

The most basic level of Rapport is physically mirroring the person you are targeting.

When you mirror someone you are simple offering that person a reflection of himself or herself. This simple technique has a super powerful impact, because of the way that people respond to their own behavior. When you offer back to your target their own behavior, they relate to it on a subconscious level and experience a sense of unity. There is little in life so satisfying as seeing a reflection of our selves in another. This is one of the most powerful tools in Ultimate Influence/Mind Control.

When you see friends at a coffee shop in conversation, chances are they are sitting in the same position, and making the same movements and gestures. If you are in a relationship (and you getting along), you and your partner will be sitting in the same physical position if you are in close proximity. You will also breathe with them.

In physics there is a law called entrainment that states those two items in motion, if in close enough proximity, they will synchronize. If you put two grandfather clocks in the same room, their pendulums will eventually swing together. This seems to also work for living creatures.

I remember being in New York City teaching this, and at the break I had a few of the student's look around the room where we were drinking coffee. You could plainly see that the people in conversations were sitting there mirror and matching each other to the point of matching all gestures and movements. They had only known each other for a few hours but had a common bond (learning mind control techniques) so they fell into natural rapport with each other. Later that day while walking to dinner with several of the students, we saw several examples of this natural event.

Two NYPD officers talking at a coffee shop, both leaning on the wall, gesturing with the hand not holding coffee.

A couple in love on a park bench in intimate conversation, there were in perfect unison in movements.

Two cab drivers in a very loud, animated conversation on directions to an address.

Since this happens in nature, let's speed up these phenomena.

What you want to do is present to your targets subconscious a mirror image of themselves, this puts your target at ease at a subconscious level, since rapport is natural in friendship, it speeds up this process. You want to first match physically your target's stance. You assume the same position as they are, sitting the same way, or standing the same way.

- Breathe at the same rate as they do.
- If they lean slightly, you lean the same way.
- They cross their legs, you cross yours.
- They adjust their clothes in some way, you adjust yours.

How is this done in a way that does not mimic them? It is easy.

1. Slow down your responses by about 3-5 seconds.

2. Keep your focus on your target, if the movement is not natural to you, it does not matter, if your target does it, you do it. If you are focused on how you feel, you are not focused on your target. Your internal state is not important, only the goal of getting rapport.

Try this as an experiment:
The next time you are in a conversation with someone and you feel you are in rapport, lean against a wall or lean back and continue talking, watch what happens. A few seconds later they will lean. Then cross your arms.... they will follow.

The more you are in rapport, the more mirroring and matching will occur. Once you are in rapport, you are in position to persuade them as you wish.

Warning!
Now that you are aware of this powerful tool, you can begin to understand why it is so important that you are careful and aware about what messages you are transmitting to your target non-verbally! If you are in rapport the people you are communicating with they will mirror your:

Frustration

Hatred

Anger

Disbelief (in them, yourself, or a product)

I stress this because we see this all the time, and in history leaders have taken societies to war by having the populace mirror their feelings. This can happen very subtly. Once while teaching a class, I received some bad news, and even though I tried to not let my anger show, the class took on a very negative tone. They were mirroring my internal state. I spend a great deal of time getting into rapport with the class, and now it was coming back at me. It renewed my respect for this technology. This points out that people will mirror their environment.

Exercises to Master Rapport

Breathing:

Mirroring someone's breathing is subtle because breathing itself is such an extremely subconscious process. When you mirror and match another person this way it is almost impossible to detect, because it is something we all have to do.

Pick some targets (people) to match breathing with in:

1. A coffee shop
2. A business meeting
3. A Party

Physical Posture:

As we stated before when people are in rapport, they mirror each other. When we do this consciously, you move into the area of gaining trust and confidence at will. To this you must practice being able to mirror and match others at will

Start in an easy place, work is where I suggest.

Pick someone you know rather well and mirror and match them in a conversation. (You are doing this anyway, but move it into the conscious level)

Pick the co-worker you know the least and start a conversation, physically mirror and match them, maintain your focus on them.

Start a conversation with your boss and do the same.

Note: Stay away from controversial subjects at this level.

Now you are ready to move into a social setting.

Start a conversation with someone in a coffee shop or restaurant and mirror and match them.

Changing with Logical Levels

Perspective is Everything!

Our brain is a vast informational system that has a series of maps. These maps grow as new information and experiences are input into our system. There is much territory around these "maps" in our brains and sometimes our perspective limits the incoming information, therefore constraining our "map". How we feel and think about things happening is a good way to explain what perspective is. Sometimes our perspective on new experiences, tasks or information can guide us in the wrong direction and it is important to make sure that we learn to control our thinking. That way we can handle change in smaller steps, making it more manageable. Smaller and manageable steps make the change seem easier therefore allowing for more confidence and being able to better handle the situation.

Logical Levels

There are different levels at which change can occur. As with anything it is easier to change things at a much lower level than one that is more complex. For example, when you think of updating your home, you think of colors, decorations and minor repairs. These are all things that are easier and will not cost an arm and leg or take much effort. The higher level remodeling jobs such as electrical, plumbing and replacing the carpet are much more difficult. Good communicator's look at the below diagram and determine the levels, then comparing to the level of change that the individual is looking for. When the levels of the diagram are all satisfied the individual is happier and more content. This can be called congruence, which is the state of the individual when they are comfortable with values and skills. Misalignment or levels that are out of order can cause individuals thought patterns to be incorrect, therefore leading to failure.

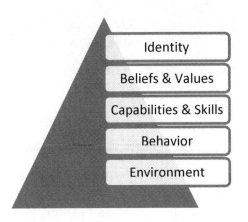

The Right Questions

When you are looking to change it is important to have a good foundation and understand of why you are changing. Sometimes answering why is the hardest part and that amazes many people. Here are the questions that you need to be asking yourself in order to determine the best plan of action and if the change is a good one. Remember the who-what-where-why and how of answering questions, well life's questions are no different.

The environment surrounding your change is very important, this is sometimes the constraining factor of change in your life. Some people are confined to the environment in which they live, sometimes it can change and other times you have to find a way around it. The environment can answer your where, when and whom questions.

Behavior involves the actions and behaviors surrounding the changes. This is the "what" question. Behavior is directly linked to the environment level.

Capabilities are about your knowledge base and how you can accomplish with your skills. Your capabilities are your guiding force and answer your how questions.

Beliefs and values are your motivational base and what allows you to begin the change itself. This is your why question and the importance associated with the change.

Identity is your sense of self and in many cases your relation to others. This is the "who" question.

Purpose is looking at the entire picture and is sometimes difficult. This is the reason and driving force behind the change as well as why it is necessary. The what for question.

Logical Levels Step by Step

One of the areas where most people go wrong is not establishing a guideline or method to their madness. Using the levels and breaking it down into smaller steps will ensure success. Think about it this way, when a person goes to climb a mountain they do not take one huge step in hopes of reaching the top. There are a series of smaller steps to get there though. Same is true in achieving goals; develop a plan and take smaller steps!

"Out of whack"

The old saying that you cannot fix what you do not acknowledge is very true. It is important to admit that a change is necessary. Whatever it may be, if you do not put a price tag on it, you will likely not adhere as closely to the steps!

The right level

After admitting there is a need for change then you must discover what level the change is needed at. Really taking inventory will help you discover the level of change that is needed. For example, is it personal, business or another area that is suffering or could improve?

Putting it into action

As with anything change in your life must come from motivation and understanding that a change could help you succeed or better your life. It's also necessary to obtain or find the right tools to help you succeed, it may be others, education, business or something else that provides the needed foundation for your change.

Uses for Logical Levels

Using logical levels can assist you in springing into action after you have answered the questions and surrounded yourself with useful tools. Here is how to use the levels in a practical and efficient manner.

INFORMATION GATHERING

Getting the facts and making use of it is very important. You wouldn't do a research paper without first gathering the information. After finding the information, organize it into a system that you can understand.

BUILDING RELATIONSHIPS

Building relationships within the family is important in a change, because it typically changes the dynamics of the entire family. Especially in changes such as marriage or divorce, where the entire family is affected. Understanding how the family can work together and implementing bonds will help continue and make the change more successful.

IMPROVE PERFORMANCE

If it is a business or personal change that is in question it is important to ensure that you are doing your best. It may be that you need to decide at what level or where the change is necessary. In business, is it a financial decision, employee morale or some other decision that is necessary.

LEADERSHIP AND CONFIDENCE

Using the levels of change is important to establish a better confidence levels and personal techniques to achieve your goals.

Finding the Tools for Change

There are certain requirements that are need for change, among these are the desire to change, knowing how to change and the opportunity for change. Deciding that you can make it happen and accepting the fact that you have choices will assist you in the change process.

* Environment

The environment and surroundings is one of the most important aspects of change. Sometimes the environment is simply not conducive to change so it makes it impossible. Instead of giving up hope, how about realigning, this will make it easier and help you achieve your goal. Changing your environment to a more conducive surrounding with people, business or friends can help make the change an easier one. For example, if you want to learn a new language it is much easier when you surround yourself with others that speak that new language.

Here are a few environmental questions to help decide the right environment choices for you: Answering questions about when you work and feel the best, types of environment where you excel and time of day that you re most successful will help place you in the right environment.

* Behavior

For the sake of communications behavior is not only your observable actions, but also the way you feel about the actions. How you feel about your behavior and actions is generally the driving forces behind the action, inspiring it again and again. It may well be the purpose that drives your behavior and until you understand that, you may have a more difficult time with changing behavior.

Determining whether or not your behavior is in line with goals is sometimes difficult, but here are a few questions that can help. Are your actions consistent with your goals, are your behaviors positive and keep you happy, is there a pattern in your behavior, if so is it consistent with your goals? What do you notice about others, are there patterns? Does your body language change in different situations? Then, note the differences.

Maximizing positive behavior is important when on the achieving path. Whether it be a salad at dinner or setting time aside for practicing that new found love for golf. For a while it is a conscious effort to maximize the right behaviors, but after a while it becomes old hat. On the flip side of that you will want to decrease bad behavior by eliminating it.

* Capabilities

Because the human mind is a learning machine it is no doubt that some people have skills or talents that are inborn. Some people seem more "capable" than others and often times others mistakenly think it is based on intelligence. Most researchers, business owners and others now realize that the best employees are those that are team oriented and have a positive attitude. Those that look at new challenges or change with a positive spirit can acquire new skills and capabilities. Just like you learn to ride a bike or snow ski, you can learn new things, if you have the desire and right attitude. Ultimate Influence looks to the learning and acquiring of new skills, but the core theory is based on the fact that all skills are learnable. Believing that employees, individuals as well as all others can learn by watching and modeling their behavior by the positive influence of others is the theory of Ultimate Influence.

Asking yourself the following questions can help you get an idea of your capabilities and help you better understand where you can make improvements. Thinking back and asking yourself about a skill that you learned at a previous time. Thinking about the events, happenings and situation that lead to the positive learning of this skill can help you recognize the pattern to make it happen again. Looking at what you are good at, what do others comment and compliment you at? Recognizing the patters and behaviors around these questions can help you focus attention leading to succeeding again.

* Beliefs & Values
    Beliefs and values drive people to either achieve their goals or be lost in trying. The way we feel about something, especially one of our goals, motivates us to continue on. Seeking out a goal is not always easy and since success does not come overnight this motivation is imperative. Our beliefs not only keep us moving toward the end result, but also help us rank our goals and wants. If there are two important things on the agenda, we have to rank and make a decision as to which to do first. Most people will move toward the goal or "thing" that has the highest price tag. For example, we may get great recognition for playing a round of golf, but if we fail to go to work, the money is shut off.

    Beliefs also keep you in the place or environment that we need to be. If our goal is to get into shape, then our goal is best achievable in the gym or fitness area. Popular belief systems state that fitness is associated with the gym, but on the other hand, we believe that "in shape and fit" is not at the ice cream parlor.

    On the levels of logics our beliefs and values drive the lower levels allowing for all of the levels to come into alignment. If you are concerned that there may be a conflict between the levels here are questions to help, make a determination. Discovering what is important to you and why, what is important to others, what do you believe to be right from wrong.

* Identity
    Many think that a person's identity is based on skills, intelligence and their behavior. Ultimate Influence looks at the definition of identity of the person separate from their behavior. Instead of lumping people into a category based on their actions, we see behavior as a consequence of an underlying motive. This belief is an optimistic view of mankind and avoids attaching labels to people based on their behavior.

    Now this does not sound like a major theory, but it is because we say a great deal about expectations of others by how we speak to them.

If we speak to someone about bad behavior and attach it to their identity, we are sending them the message that their character is flawed. We need to speak about the behavior and avoid negative affect to the identity level of the individual.

Here are questions to answer if there is conflict surrounding identity. How do you express yourself, how do you feel about yourself, how do others feel about you, do you label others, do others have an accurate picture of who you really are?

* Purpose
The purpose or reason behind is generally the reason in which people journey onward to their goal. For some people their purpose is larger than their identity and they achieve great things. People journey through life sometimes questioning their purpose in life, but it is often right in front of them. They are looking too hard! Through hard times and great suffering, there have been individuals that have persevered because their passion was greater than any other thing in their life. Look at Dalai Lama and the resistance, suffering, but the passion was definitely a driving force, some might say the only force.

A passion for something will generally keep an individual on track for much longer than normal. People will endure great things when they feel strongly about something. Finding a passion or purpose will guide a person toward their goal regardless of the conflict or troubles that they cross during their journey. Answering the following questions will help with your purpose. What are you here on Earth for, how do you want people to remember you when you die, what strengths can you use to contribute to a higher good?

Recognizing other peoples Logical Levels

By recognizing other people's comments you can determine their logical levels and/or conflict. Being able to determine the level of the individual will enable you to help them make the necessary changes. Also understanding that it is not always what they say, but where the emphasis is placed in the sentence. Here are some statements and evaluations:

The Fundamental Sentence

Mastering the art of persuasion means learning every trick in this book, and more. If you want results now, you can start by memorizing the fundamental sentence. Don't worry. Humans only want to learn the basics at first.

When the jargon and intricacies of the material available are stripped away, one is left with a basic, but sound understanding. It might manifest in different ways, but what is important is to grasp it fully, so that your new wisdom will be available at a moment's notice.

What you are about to read underpins every successful usage of persuasion. You can't escape it if you want to influence something. If you memorize these words and the truth to them, you can start applying them to your daily life. You may notice desirable results that may have eluded you for years.

"People will do anything for those who encourage their dreams, justify their failures, allay their fears, confirm their suspicions and help them throw rocks at their enemies."

A wise person would read this sentence repeatedly, and reflect on its meaning. This book is the science of persuasion, boiled down to the very core. It contains information on the five key aspects of high influence, as outlined by Blair Warren's 2005 report.

- Encouragement of Dreams
- Justification of Failures
- Allaying Fears
- Confirming Suspicions
- Throwing Rocks at Enemies

As previously discussed, persuasion is not a hard science. This sentence wasn't summoned up in a laboratory and drafted into an obscurely forced academic paper. This sentence highlights one of the deepest aspects of human nature that we all intuitively understand, and uses these elements to create tools that can be applied today.

What you've just read isn't new. It isn't the latest in persuasion research. Often people pretend to have new secrets but dress them up as common sense or simple practice, to make a profit. Understand that you don't need dozens of books, if you can empathize with the notion of the *fundamental sentence* contained in this book.

The *fundamental sentence* is a tool that can be applied immediately and has great power behind it.

Magic Words

And The Fundamental Sentence

When we think of *magic words*, phrases like *abracadabra*, or *hocus pocus* come to mind. Magicians use these words to create an air of awe, to draw attention, and to lull an audience into an atmosphere of mystery that the magician is creating.

It is important to have a broader definition of *magic words* if we are to use them in fundamental science. Defined - *magic words* are any words that can create power.

Think of the rules of etiquette as an example.

Children are taught that if they memorize and use *magic words*, then when they ask for things, they'll get what they want and that others around them will think better of them, and this is true. Having manners and being polite can do a lot in the way of persuasion. Simple manners go a long way because most people forget to use them regularly.

A more complicated example of the use of *magic words* is seen in the main religions. While most religions don't practice in the occult or use any magical practices, rituals and prayers still hold power, through belief, faith, and hope.

Religious people consider their prayers to keep power, but prayers only hold power within individuals.

The words spoken in prayer seem other-worldly when compared to everyday conversation. It shouldn't be surprising to know that many *magic words* used by magicians hold their roots within religious doctrines.

Christians, Muslims, Buddhists, and Hindus each have their words of power, and each religion holds their individual magic words at a level of high significance. The majority of people around the world put a lot of their faith under the terms of the authority figures within their religion. Religion can bring people together, allowing them to become a part of something greater than themselves, and serve an ideal larger than themselves.

To tap into a person's need for ethical approval, or approval from a higher power is a technique often used by magicians. It is closely tied to our need for wonderment.

Magic words are meant to get something done. If they didn't have a believed effect, no one would have any respect or reverence for them. If a magician uses *magic words* during his performance, the audience expects something to happen, and they expect a result.

For the master of persuasion, a magic word is one that achieves influence over the other person. It isn't magic. The faith that people put into words creates a sense of magic. Knowing someone well means knowing what words are magic to them.

In hypnosis and psychotherapy, there are also *magic words* that can reveal information. The way someone chooses to describe their personal life, their work, or their family, can determine a great deal about them without any need for further detail.

NLP and Trance Words

NLP, Neuro-Linguistic Programming, is a tool people use to change how they behave through language and conscious effort. In the scientific world, its validity is sometimes referred to as being dubious, but many have claimed that NLP methods have completely changed their lives for the better.

In our pursuit of knowledge of the art of persuasion, it is important to examine its importance in NLP.

NLP requires that you know what you want. You have to get the attention of your unconscious mind, and you have to know what you are going to see inside yourself. Through intention and techniques, people have used NLP to succeed in various endeavors like conquering addiction or becoming a better speaker.

One aspect of NLP includes *trance words*. While in a conversation, listen to someone as they talk about something that is important to them, such as their job, their relationships with friends and family, or a hobby. Take particular note of the words they repeat. These are their personal *trance words*. NLP teaches that these words are deeply connected to the unconscious mind. By understanding someone's *trance words*, gaining influence over them can be simple.

If you were talking to someone, who was deeply religious and used words like "bless" and "holy" seamlessly in conversation, for example, that person will likely feel drawn to others who use the same vocabulary. You can adjust your vocabulary to suit your needs, simply by listening to the words of others before you speak.

In "48 Laws of Power," Robert Greene states that *"By holding up a mirror to their psyches, you seduce [others] with the illusion that you share their values; by holding up a mirror to their actions, you teach them a lesson."*

Understanding *trance words* and how to use them is a form of mirroring. People like to reflect on their values as well as how they are seen by others. Everyone assumes their way of viewing the world is the right way, and when that opinion is outwardly reflected by someone else, trust comes naturally.

As you can see, this is just another form of confirming suspicions and appealing to dreams. *Trance words* are a prime example of the real world application of the *fundamental sentence*. If what you want happens to mirror what others want, you have taken a step in convincing someone to manifest your will.

The Fundamental Sentence in Practice
Basic History

Throughout history, the fundamental truths of persuasion have grown to be more and more critical. Since the beginning of civilization, there has been a need for those in power to control others. In ancient times, persuasion wasn't as necessary as it is now. Kings and tyrants often relied heavily on military might, coercion, and primal brutality for their success. While it was sometimes wise to appeal to people's human nature at that time, the technique rarely worked out. In trading and bartering on a world scale, for example, armies could decimate whole populations who didn't agree with their economics.

The truths of persuasion found their roots within parts of society that were more stable. On the frontiers and in war, it was instinctual to fight and survive, and this instinct dominated. In populated areas, and in areas where war was distant, it grew to be crucial for people of all classes to be able to convince and persuade, as opposed to pillaging.

In essence, as civilization grows, so does the importance of our *fundamental sentence.*

In ancient Athens, where the first democratic system was founded, persuasion was considered to be respected and studied intensely. The Athenians believed that the most important traits of a politician were rhetoric and elocution. They wanted leaders who could speak their mind openly and convince the masses.

As civilizations around the world have progressed, the more advanced they have become, and the more necessary has become as a result. Barbarians relied on brutality and violence. Think of the last time a politician promised death to all who opposed him. This technique is no longer wise as history has shown, but persuasion can still be used for evil purposes if the masses can be influenced.

When we look at the effects of persuasion from the most recent global dictators of the 20th Century, we see that some leaders often use NLP techniques to convince the masses.

During the Russian Civil War, Lenin and Bolsheviks blamed 'rich peasants,' for hoarding precious grain and causing the food shortages during the war. Lenin needed food for his troops and for the cities to maintain his support, so he used this technique to feed his army regardless of the cost.

With a scapegoat at hand, the Red Army Soldiers felt no remorse when they ventured out into the countryside and stole all the grain they could from the peasants. In reality, the shortage of food was due to poor planning in regards to The Civil War, but the soldiers could not be persuaded as such. As consequence of the war and the thieving Red Army, Russia experienced one of the worst famines in human history. People starved to death, by the millions.

How did this happen?

Both the people in the cities and the soldiers had their suspicions confirmed, that there were people hoarding food other than themselves, eating plentifully, while they were left hungry. With an enemy at hand, Lenin let his soldiers "throw stones at them", by overlooking their traveling out into the countryside and raiding where they could, in a wave of manic barbarianism.

Hitler and his appeals to the dreams of the German people are another good examples. World War I had brought shameful defeat for the Germans, made worse by the seemingly harsh conditions of the Treaty of Versailles.

The people dreamed of a time of prosperity and pride, where their land would be restored again to a state of greatness. Hitler capitalized on this desire and told the German people exactly what they wanted to hear, before using them to carry out his will.

Hitler appealed to the darker parts of the German people as well. His rise and reign are marked with a clear distinction between 'us' and 'them.' Hitler justified the failures of the German people, blaming the failure of World War I on many groups, the Communists, the Liberal politicians and famously, the Jewish people. Again we see how profoundly our *fundamental sentence* affects human nature? Hitler calmed fears with grand promises of a better future, and he confirmed suspicions by pointing the finger at countries externally, and minorities internally. With these enemies created in the public mind, Hitler and his party encouraged the Germans to resort to violence against any Communists and Jewish people within the borders of Germany.

Luckily, positive people also appeal to human nature to get what they want. Many civil and religious leaders in history have employed the ideas behind the *fundamental sentence* to change the world for the better. Martin Luther King Jr's "I Have A Dream" speech is summarized by its first words. He spoke sincerely about the future and dreams of his people, and many other demographic groups within the United States, creating a mass of change with a few hundred words.

People of high power understand that influence is in their grasp. The study of any great leader or dictator throughout history leads to the conclusion that most have employed some aspect of the fundamental sentence in their endeavors.

In more contemporary examples, you don't have to look far to see the mark of the *fundamental sentence*. Politicians, salesman, marketing executives, leaders, and even con artists understand the importance of human nature. This understanding is effortlessly expressed through the *fundamental sentence*. In trying to find a successful ad campaign that does not utilize one or more of these five insights, one may not ever find success.

Barack Obama led a brilliant campaign in 2008, promising "Hope and Change." The Bush administration had left on a sour note, and with the economic crisis lingering, the people hungered for hope and change. Obama's "Hope and Change" speech appealed to the human nature within the American people, who wanted their quality of life to be better.

Barack Obama was able to capitalize on the people's desire for change, a change from a conservative government to liberal, as well as a change in tradition and acceptance by becoming the first black president of The United States. The perception was that if he were able to win the election, doors would open for a new period in the history of The United States, a time where any citizen, regardless of race, can win a seat in the highest office in the country.

Hope and Change

The year 2016 witnessed Donald Trump's capitalization on the vein of human nature.

Make America Great Again.

That alone is a promise that holds power in the human mind. It appeals to the pride that Americans feel toward their country, their deep patriotism. It promises a return to what once made America Great, whatever the individual considers that to be.

Donald Trump's rhetoric appealed to the masses. He didn't self-censor. More than that, Donald Trump spoke of immigration, the outsourcing of jobs, and a global lack of respect. He talked about dreams and promised to relieve fears if he was awarded the honor of attaining government office.

People in the *Rust Belt* were especially convinced. Traditionally a wall of Democrat support, they were turned by the appeal of Donald's strong words. They had lost countless jobs, and they were feeling left in the cold by a political party that they were used to relying on for their interests. With their support, Donald Trump secured his presidency.

Another way Donald Trump achieved his win was by creating *us vs. them* scenario. Donald Trump called out media intolerance and bias, as well as the elite and the wealthy, who he claimed to think, were exploiting the American people. Often at campaign rallies, he would point towards the cameras and label them the "Dishonest Press," while his supporters turned, booing and throwing insults at the videographers. In the mind of a Trump supporter, Hillary Clinton represented the pinnacle of privilege, corruption, and special treatment, while Donald Trump was an honest, say-anything type. He was the man who was claiming to fix the entire political system.

Donald ensured that his speeches appealed to the masses. He would say the things that other people were too afraid to say. Trump promised everything that the working class wanted. Without a brilliant understanding of the nature of human beings, their actions and reactions, Donald Trump's campaign would have failed, as many hoped it would when he announced it initially.

Don't just look to the Presidents of our modern age. Think deeply about the advertisements that bombard your senses every hour of the day as well. All marketing tries to appeal to at least one of the five insights within the *fundamental sentence*. These insights have a strange hold on our everyday lives without our even knowing it.

Perhaps one of the most infamous examples of the use of the *fundamental sentence* was in the book, "The Secret," written by Rhonda Byrne. Aimed at people who found their lives to be lacking in some way, this book used the techniques of persuasion very effectively. In summary, "The Secret," claims that positive thinking will cause positive outcomes and that negative thinking will cause negativity to manifest. While there is some objective truth to this, the book pushes beyond just positive thinking and delves into dangerous territory.

Firstly, the book claims that your dreams and ambitions can be realized, if you apply its principles, keep those thoughts in mind, and reject the negative. This aspect of the book appeals to the selfish part of human nature, in which our will for happiness is put above everything else. The book encourages the reader's dreams, while also ensuring that they are reliant on the book to achieve their goals.

Then, the book makes clear that it isn't anybody's fault if goals have not yet been realized, because they have not yet learned "The Secret." The book insists that there is no need to blame oneself for missing out so far and that all will now be well with the book in hand.

It also reinforces the idea that without "The Secret," people would be just as lost and hopeless as they were before. The book builds a dependency with the reader so that they will only be able to develop their goals in the way in which they are told.

"The Secret" suggests that everyone who is wealthy and successful knows something that others don't, that the wealthy are intent on keeping others down.

You can see from its success just how compelling a book like "The Secret," can be. By tuning into the deepest parts of human nature, people are convinced that its information is some of the absolute truth. The *fundamental sentence* underlies every success in the practice of persuasion. Without the essential ideas held within the *fundamental sentence*, there is little hope that you will be able to express your will onto the world in the way that you want to.

On Encouraging Their Dreams...

As discussed earlier, we all have a will. We all have a strong idea of how we want our world to look. Since childhood, we were taught that we can't always get what we want, and we have had to come to terms with that. Parents often discourage the dreams of their children for what they think is their good, and attempt to steer them toward more attainable goals. The average person faces the word 'no' on a regular basis and considers the use of the word to be normal. When someone cares about the dreams of another and more than that, are willing to help make them happen, others perk up and listen. Logic takes a back seat when someone promises the world.

Robert Cialdini once mentioned a relevant example in his career. Along with a group of others, he witnessed a sales pitch for *Transcendental Meditation*, where some of the promised results were far beyond the realm of reality. At the end of the pitch, Robert's friend pointed out all the logical flaws in the program, and others had little to rebuke his logic. To Robert's surprise, much of the audience was willing to sign up, and pay, despite the program's flaws. Upon investigation, he found it was because his friend had scared these people. The meditation had promised to fix the problems that these people had, and when the flaws were pointed out, they worried that soon they'd be having the same doubts. Prospective customers took a leap of faith, in hopes that their problems would be solved, and ultimately made the purchase.

On Justifying Their Failures...

It's deep within human nature to not take responsibility for our mistakes. It is most evident in children who say anything to avoid getting in trouble. Many adults act in the same way. It is a mark of a highly devolved person to step up and take ownership for their mistakes, although no one enjoys doing so. Millions of people are looking for a way out - they don't want anything to be their fault, they don't want to be responsible for the bed that they sleep in. To be adept at persuasion, you must be able to own up to your mistakes but to have influence over others you need to ease their pain while turning it to your advantage.

Think of the last time someone made you feel responsible for a shortcoming of yours. How co-operative do you say you were with that person? When we have to face our weaknesses, we want to run and hide. If someone manages to turn that towards us, making it our responsibility, we are automatically more receptive towards them.

On Allaying Their Fears...

Fear is a negative and powerful emotion, but unlike depression or apathy, fear moves people into action. When afraid, people find it hard to concentrate on anything other than what is causing their fear. It is well known in psychology and the world of common sense that an insecure person will often seek out a much more dominant partner to relieve their fear of making decisions or being in charge. While such relationships seem one-sided, both parties are usually satisfied with the outcome. Choose to be the person in charge, who is ready to show everyone else the way, and allay their fears.

The mainstream media has mastered the art of using fear to create a reaction. Next time you are watching the news, pay attention to how certain stories make you feel, and what actions they make you want to take. Ads can also take a similar route, by presenting you with a problem that makes you feel fearful. Luckily, as television representatives will tell you, there is a solution. This method of sales involves a fundamental problem, reaction, and solution formula that is commonly used in marketing.

On Confirming Their Suspicions...

Something we have already assumed to be proven correct creates high satisfaction while reinforcing belief. There is nothing quite like having suspicions confirmed. A relationship of trust can be built through one person's actions - confirming what the other had suspected all along. Simply put, we like to be right.

In the 1950s, the United States could not stop thinking about communist threat. Double agents had leaked information to the Soviets about the atomic bomb, and the Soviets had begun building their weapons. Joseph McCarthy capitalized on this widespread suspicion by claiming that many members of the State Department and the Administration of Henry S. Truman were communist spies. While later events took a different turn for McCarthy, at the time the notoriety and publicity of his accusations brought him into the public spotlight as one of the people's champions.

On Helping Them Throw Rocks At Their Enemies...

Adversity creates allies.

"The enemy of my enemy is my friend."

When there is a clear distinction made between "us" and "them," those who are in the "us" group, benefit from a feeling of inclusion. The idea behind persuasion is to display yourself as if you are in the "us" group. It is important to understand that most people have enemies and a clear example of "us vs. them" in their lives. When someone is engaged in a struggle, they are looking for others to join in. Those who do, become more than friends. Those who do become life partners.

Like magic, these five insights hold an incredible power. We may be disillusioned when we discover the simplicity of a magic trick, but the magician is not. The magician understands the power of simplicity. Magicians take simple secrets that wouldn't fool anybody when exposed and build upon them to create illusions that baffle some of the most brilliant minds.

It is the same with the power of persuasion. The effects can be so life-altering that we remain convinced that there has to be something deeper. More often than not, there is, in fact, nothing more profound for which to look. There is simply the correct application of basic principles by people who appreciate their power.

Principles are more important than strategies because strategies cannot exist without principles.

A good thing to remember is that if you understand the principles of persuasion, you can adapt to any situation, whereas with techniques and strategies, you may only be able to navigate a few specific situations.

History was made by great leaders who have manipulated people into doing their bidding. You are vulnerable if you have a desire that overrides your logic. Perhaps this section is best concluded with the words of a con man.

"Everyone is willing to give you something. They're ready to give you something for whatever it is they're hungry for." - Henry Oberlander

43

What's Missing?

There is something else worth noting about the *fundamental sentence*. It is missing something that most people think is crucial to the persuasion process.

Read the sentence again:

"People will do anything for those who encourage their dreams, justify their failures, allay their fears, confirm their suspicions and help them throw rocks at their enemies."

You are omitted from this sentence. Don't mistake this as saying that you don't matter, however.

The painful truth is that most people won't care about you. People usually only genuinely care about themselves. Don't judge others, and this is human nature. Instead, try to understand that people will instinctively put their interests first, and only their desires will move them toward the action you want.

Any advertisement that puts the company's long history, before serving the customers need, is not going to have many customers. People who want to succeed with others know this and put forth extra time and effort into actually understanding the other person's motives. These are the individuals who can better serve themselves and push towards their goals.

Coming to this realization is sad, but it seems that this is just the way the world is. Deep down, people care more about their gain than they do about others. They feel only Stheir hunger, and will only listen to people who can help them in some way.

Surround yourself with people who make you feel good *about yourself.* Two people must both be mutually serving each other's interests, in any relationship. The business world holds the same notion - businesses give the customer what they need, and the customer provides the company money and growth. One cannot function without the other.

People who seem more concerned with their gain above those of others make themselves less desirable to be around. Companies who seem ruthless in their hunt for profit make consumers not want to purchase from them. If you want to have some skill in the art of persuasion, you need to understand that the focus of others is never on you.

It is not difficult to understand these strategies. One on one encounters with others are the easiest situations in which to practice the ideas behind the *fundamental sentence*. Review the history of persuasion and inform yourself as to how the principles are used in other contexts, such as in websites and advertising.

A while ago, two friends launched a website that obliterated sales records. Their success surprised everyone involved, and there was much discussion as to why their project was so effective.

People wanted to know why this had worked for the pair. Had they chosen the right product and price? Or was it just the right time?

After examination, it was clear that their copy appealed to basic human needs.

Some headlines explicitly encourage the thought of being free, but they can also subliminally claim that the answer doesn't always lie within the reader, but rather something else. This approach takes the reader "off the hook" while maintaining confirmation of suspicions that there may be an easy answer to life's dilemmas, available for purchase.

Justifying the failure of others is one of the keys aspects of the *fundamental sentence*. In his book, *Forbidden Keys to Persuasion*, Blair Warren refers to this as "scapegoating." While the terminology here may be different, the underlying principle is the same.

Scapegoating is a commonly used technique in media advertising. The media often attempts to convince viewers that their problems are not their fault, that their problems will go away with the simple purchase of a product. People sometimes feel more comfortable when assuming no responsibility for actions or reactions. Business owners, salespeople, and marketing executives know how to frame a problem in such a way that it doesn't reflect poorly on the consumer.

Consider an independent contractor who is used to meeting potential clients in their homes, and often notices their embarrassment as to the condition or cleanliness of where they live. If this contractor has mastered the art of persuasion, he will point out that these problems may be the fault of something beyond the client's control. As a result of this affirmative action, the number of quotes that the contractor receives will increase significantly. This is example shows just how widespread and applicable our *fundamental sentence* can be. Most people think that they are above these core principles, or don't have the curiosity to care. These sorts of people will remain without the vital knowledge that everyone wants to have a chance in the game that is played while trying to form human relationships.

For this type of persuasion to be effective, they need to fit seamlessly into the context of the message. Like magic, when the mechanics are revealed to the audience, the wonder disappears. Persuasion doesn't mean keeping your motives entirely hidden. Instead, persuasion ensures that the behavior seems natural.

People don't like to have their weaknesses used to the advantage of someone else. If you want to obtain influence over someone, you can't let it seem like you want to control them.

Readers of this book must remember to use what they have learned in an ethical way. People do not deserve to be lied to, or manipulated into negative situations. Your persuasion should be practiced with moral integrity.

Unsurprisingly, if you are genuine *and* persuasive, your success will increase hugely.

Bringing It All Together

I wish I could tell you that you are now a master of persuasion, but it is the basics of human nature that need to be understood before achieving this title. Using the *fundamental sentence* as a platform, we have uncovered and discovered what it is that makes people turn thoughts into actions.

It has been demonstrated that everyone has their will or the way that they would individually like the world to be. Many people haven't yet developed the right skills or mindset to achieve their goals, but some people realize that they can turn their dreams into a reality through persuasion. Persuasion is one of the skills that is necessary for success.

The backbone of the report has been the *fundamental sentence:*

"People will do anything for those who encourage their dreams, justify their failures, allay their

fears, confirm their suspicions and help them throw rocks at their enemies."

Reworded:

The art of persuasion involves convincing others of your ability to be compassionate, and persuasion can be achieved most effectively through positive actions.

This reworded sentence captures the very essence of persuasion in a way that you may be more likely to remember. By remembering this one sentence, you are already better equipped than most people will ever be.

Magic and magicians have a clear understanding of this sentence, even if it is only intuitively. To be able to create, speculate, and wonder with simplicity is the essence of the *fundamental sentence*. NLP is known to be demonstrated as one of the best methods of hacking into human nature and the psyche of the mind. *Trance words* are like a fast-forward into a person's mind and can be used to leverage your will onto the world as well.

The history of persuasion cannot be overlooked as well. If someone devotes time to the study of history, that person will find

49

wisdom and truth that they can practice in their daily routines. With history comes the study of war, culture, art, and people. Individuals have shown us that it is easy to choose temptation over pure, hard logic over the course of time.

We can see examples of persuasion in our everyday lives, from Donald Trump to best-selling novels, and these models reaffirm the truth of the *fundamental sentence*. Today, people use magic to sell things, to cause others to act in their best interests, and to create real action in the world. Even in ancient Greece, it was essential for any leader or person of authority to have a grip on human nature.

With the *Fundamental Sentence* broken down, we can see how each aspect of the sentence is personified. It may pass under our radars every day without our realizing it, but the art of persuasion is always at work. Being mindful and aware means not getting caught off guard by things that use human nature against your best interests.

Examples in business and adverting have been used to show these very same principles, and we now know that persuasion means keeping "you" out of the equation. Use these thoughts in real world applications.

The *fundamental sentence* is a hallmark reminder that it is the principles of skill that do all the hard lifting in life, as opposed to the strategies that come about as a result. Human nature has remained constant for the history of humankind. We care about our self-interests and our gains above all else. This notion can be extended to family, community, or nation. Donald Trump called to this when he said "America First," as a salesman appeals to it when he offers health insurance to protect your family in the case of an accident.

Understanding how we operate and what drives us into action makes us strong as people. Don't be conned into a bad deal when you have a full grip on human nature.

Throughout this book, we have covered the underlying nature of persuasion. This art should now be clear, so you can start applying it today. If you want to advance your successes with others, you'll take these principles to heart.

HUMAN Needs

My dear friend Anthony Robbins introduced the idea of The Six Human Needs. Having developed a lifelong interest in human behavior, development and motivation he studied many models of therapy including Neuro Linguistic Programming, Cognitive Therapy, Gestalt Therapy combined with Maslow's Hierarchy of Needs. Robbins combined elements from Maslow's Hierarchy of Needs with his own discoveries to determine what guides and motivates our decisions and actions.

Maslow's Hierarchy of Needs explores:

- Physiological Needs
- Safety Needs
- Love and Belonging Needs
- Esteem Needs
- Self-Actualization

Maslow's pyramid of needs demonstrates how our needs change as we progress up the hierarchy.

On the bottom of the hierarchy we have the physiological needs for breathing, food, water, sex, sleep, excretion etc. As these needs are satisfied we move up the pyramid to satisfy safety needs such as security of the self, of the family, property, health and employment. Next is the need for love and belonging and how we connect with people through family, friendship and sexual relationship. We then seek out our esteem needs to boost self-esteem, confidence, achievement and respect from others. The top of the pyramid is the need for self-actualization where we desire self-improvement through creativity and helping to make the world a better place.

Maslow's Hierarchy of Needs focused on personal growth and contribution but Robbins felt it didn't explain why we do what we do. He then developed the six core "Human Needs" that each of us works to satisfy on a mostly unconscious level.

The needs move in an ascending order ranging from personality, material levels to encompassing connectivity, interaction and our energetic influence in the world.

The focus for our prioritized need may be different depending on our various phases and areas of life. Each need serves as a fundamental part of creating a life that is whole and fulfilling at all levels.

The Six Human Needs are:

1. Certainty

Each of us has a need at a basic level to accomplish a primary sense of stability in the world. The need for certainty revolves around us doing what we need to feel safe, secure and in control ranging from paying our bills, having a roof over our heads to feeling comfortable with our relationships. We value predictability in order to avoid stress, anxiety and worry. As the world and the lives of those around us is constantly changing, satisfying this need can be challenging as we continue to control and resist change to stay in our comfort zone. We either find certainty by seeking it externally or by trying to control others or we can take responsibility to find more certainty within to gaining a greater level of self-worth. The human need for certainty becomes more positive when we trust that everything is changing. Alternatively, if we have too much certainty in our lives we may begin to feel bored and dissatisfied. We then seek out more variety.

2. Variety/Uncertainty

To allow ourselves to evolve we have a need for uncertainty to break the habits of predictability. Variety provides us with new interests, challenges, surprises and adventure through making changes in our life in order to feel more alive. We take more risks letting go of needing to know the outcome. Variety and certainty sit on either side of a scale and are very much connected to each other. The scale needs to be in constant balance as too much uncertainty can lead to stress and overwhelm and then we seek certainty to regain comfort and more predictability. The cycle continues as we seek to find balance between running on automatic in our comfort zones to wanting to break up the monotony and desire more interest and change in our lives.

3. Significance

As we balance the polarities of certainty and variety we want to be seen and supported for who we are and what we do in the world. We all have a need to feel important, different and unique. We want to feel special in some way that makes us feel significant. Significance is the quality of being worthy and forms part of creating a sense of identity for how we show up in the world. We seek a sense of accomplishment through the goals we set, the skills we develop and the status we attain. In seeking out our need for significance we constantly compare ourselves and become dependent on the approval of others to feel good within ourselves. If we become dependent on the input from others to fulfill our need for significance it can be very challenging. Rather than relying on the approval of others to feel complete within ourselves we can fulfill the need for significance through connecting with our own path of integrity, having more compassion and giving more to others.

4. Love and Connection

To experience fulfillment in life we all have a need to love and be loved by others. We want to feel like we belong. In seeking our need for significance we feel we have to be different than everyone but this conflicts with the need for connection and love. We can temporarily feel satisfied with our achievements trying to stand out and be unique but we will feel disconnected.

Significance, love and connection need to be in constant balance as they sit on either side of the scale. By having too much significance we feel too different and look for change. We need to love others and connect with them by letting go of our uniqueness. If we take time to connect to our Self and love the aspects of our being this genuine connection infuses out into the world to others.

The first four Human Needs are centered on our individual quest for self-fulfillment and achievement. They are more fundamental personality needs that are in a constant strive for balance. The last two needs provide doorways that help and support each other to achieve a greater level of fulfillment in life.

5. Growth

The need for growth isn't a fundamental need or a need that all people strive to fulfil. We may feel comfortable and have some level of uncertainty, we might feel significant and meet our need for connection but without growth there will be a sense of dissatisfaction or stagnation because we are not evolving. Growth can take place in a number of ways but importantly it is about self-reflection and being both aware and responsible for our actions and choices.

6. Contribution

The positive fulfilment of the other five needs sees the rise of the need for contribution. Contribution means living our life's purpose and bringing something to the world to benefit others or giving value for something greater than ourselves. Our need for contribution comes from a desire to have our lives mean something by being of service to the world. This need might be fulfilled through a business, volunteering or taking time to smile or help someone in need. Contribution is not just about what we do but also about who we are being in the world.

Growth and contribution support each other as when we contribute to others we have the opportunity to grow. By growing we increase our capacity to give and make a difference in the world. By fulfilling our need for growth we understand that it is a journey and it means allowing ourselves to become more authentic and to share what we learn with others. True meaning in life is experienced through contributing beyond ourselves.

The Six Human Needs help us to understand the needs we endeavor to fulfil each day. As we recognize the choices we make and the incentive for our behaviors we can move towards experiencing a life of meaning and purpose.

Review The Six Human Needs in Your Life by:

- Becoming more aware of your thought patterns, behaviors, actions and decisions.
- How do you currently satisfy your basic needs?
- Do you focus more on one or two human needs?
- Do you feel that one of the Human Needs requires more focus or attention?
- How do you currently prioritize your needs and are they in alignment with the way you choose to live your life?

By regularly reviewing the Six Human Needs you can use them to guide and motivate you to focus on creating more balance and moving towards a more fulfilling life.

You need to look at how what you want fits into your targets human needs.

If you fill 3 of the four basic needs they will follow you or your advice as it helps them fit their model of the world.

Sub Modalities: How to Focus Your Brain for Optimum Results

Have you ever noticed that people react to the same situation much differently? One person can welcome a challenge with open arms and feel empowered while another will crumble with the pressure. These "states" of mind are built around your internal representation and physiology, defined by experiences. Experiences help us form our internal representation and how we perceive what is going on around us. The way we embrace new challenges can be changed by how we focus on things and what we focus on. Read on to find out how to take charge of our focusing ability.

Focusing Attention in a Situation

There are millions of stimuli thrown at the brain at any one second. The brain acts as a filter and sorts through these stimuli determining what is most urgent or needs attention. The brain works through a information process known as "chunking", which is basically the ability to group certain memories together for ready recall. For example, it may be the memory of a high school play is associated with the musty smelling cologne of a history teacher and the way he twirled his mustache. Now there were several other behaviors, actions and environments happening at the time, but these are the pieces that the brain (memory) has chunked together.

Now think about it from a point of failure in your life. Most people recall this information and replay the "failing" moments over and over again. Instead of turning this information into feedback and learning they begin to feed negative thoughts into their heads. How successful do you think this makes the person? Not very, in fact it sets them up for failure. The question then becomes, "how do I change this state and look at experiences in a positive light"? The answer is a change in the way you focus on things. Instead of always picking off the negative or how you screwed something up, turn it and replay the situation with a more positive note. Imagine that the "screw up" was resolved and see yourself succeeding. What you are doing is changing how you focus on things.

After the years of a negative internal script you will have to remain constant in redirecting your focus to the positive, but stay with it. After programming a negative focus and internal script for years our brains go on auto pilot and automatically begins feeding into the situation at hand. This take a little bit to change; the internal scripting has to become positive just as it became negative. After a while the mind will change to a positive auto pilot mode. It takes work, but it can be done.

Directing Our Focus

Our internal scripting is based on not only what we think, but also how we feel. It is possible to create a mental image to motivate and draw focus to a particular scenario. As we have already found in life, the intensity of a state of mind is based on the intensity of the situation or picture in our mind. Now that all sounds confusing, but you will see from this example; most people feel motivated to go shopping, but sometimes it is more intense than others, right? This is because of our mental images about the situation. Shopping may not be as much fun because there are issues such as money, time and finding the right piece of clothing. But, imagine yourself shopping for anything you want with a $50,000 gift certificate you just won. Does that change the scenario? Of course it does, it is a bigger, clearer and brighter picture in your mind. Visualization can change the state by the mere intensity of the pictures in the mind. This is because the mind is drawn to a bigger, more distinct set of pictures of circumstances. Many say that this could be considered excitement. The pictures in our mind oftentimes are automatically populated, leaving us with little control. This can however, be changed. The way to rectify this is to focus on positive pictures and images (of success) making a mental movie, eventually the mind will begin automatically populating with more positive images.

What is meant by more intense pictures is what you see in the movies, think about it. The colors, sounds, light and angles all add to the intensity and desire of the movie. If the picture is small, colors are dim and the angle is off, would it be as interesting? NO!

The Keys to the Brain

The brain is often referred to as one large operating computer. The sub modalities or "keys" to the mind allows you to control actions, thoughts and perceptions. These sub modalities are classified into three categories: visual, auditory and kinesthetic. Let's look at the three sub modalities and their input, because in order to understand our state, we must understand the coding system of the brain.

- The visual sub modalities are how your brain codes pictures or sights. Think about looking at a picture the same things that you notice in a picture is what your brain is coding about what you are physically looking at. Is the picture focused or out of focus, what is the location of the item in the picture is it framed or panoramic and is it disassociated or associated?
- The auditory sub modalities are the way the brain codes sounds. Just as if you hear a sound you can separate it into different categories. Is it loud or soft, slow or fast, in tune or out of tune?
- Kinesthetic sub modalities are the brains coding of internal feelings. This is one of the more difficult coding systems to understand, because it is not always as clear cut. Separations of things such as the location of the feeling, still or moving, light or heavy and the direction of movement are all taken into consideration in the coding process.

Coding and internal scripting is different for everyone. Finding the way that your brain codes and creates a particular situation is a discovery process and is a very important step towards success.

Disassociation & Association

There are two types of image coding of the brain; disassociation and association. To demonstrate the two types of coding a good example is the easiest way to understand. When you visualize a past event or situation in your life, do you see yourself at a distance or through your own eyes? If you are seeing the situation from a distance, this is disassociation. When you visualize the event from your own eyes this is association. We tend to visualize negative events from a distance or as a disassociation and positive events with association. The association or disassociation can have a great impact on one's state of mind and here is why.

Close your eyes and remember back to a positive event in your life, anything that you want it to be. Remember the location, smells, sounds and who is there with you. Visualize through your own eyes and walk through the experience once again. This inspires a good and positive feeling. Now take that same situation and visualize from a distance (disassociation). You are basically stepping out of your body and removing yourself from the events. Do you see how the mood and state changes? It has a great impact, because the more involved we are with a positive feeling the better "state" the person will be in.

Ability to Intensify any State

Speaking of a magic wand, wouldn't it be great to be able to intensify or replicate a feeling or state immediately on cue. Unfortunately, no one has developed this wand so we have to come up with another way to intensify a positive state. Intensifying involves shifting the sub modalities and here is how:

- Imagine and visualize a goal that you want to achieve, but have not found the motivation to achieve.
- Close your eyes and visualize yourself achieving that goal. Take notes about all the sub modalities involved in the experience. Make mental notes of whether the situation is disassociated or associated, sounds, feelings, the shape of the feeling (light, heavy or movement),
- Rate the sub modalities on a scale of 1-10, with ten being the amount of motivation and intensity you felt as you stood in achievement of your goal.

Mapping Across Love to Disgust

Feeling differently about a situation can be done and it is a matter of shifting your sub modalities. There are steps to changing motivation to un-motivation or love to disgust. Of course it is great to be able to change an unmotivated goal to a motivated goal, but the reverse is sometimes necessary as well. Think about when you are motivated for that bowl of ice cream that is a whopping 500 calories. In order to achieve your dream weight, you must unmotivated quickly, here is the five steps to control motivation.

Step One: Elicit the sub modalities of a food you love

Imagine a food that is not the healthiest choice, but one you really want. Now make mental notes about the sub modalities. Most of them involve kin esthetics, because it is a substance. Imagine the smell, feel and most of all the taste. Rate all the things that you like about this type of food from 1-10, since you like this food it should be up toward 10.

Step Two: Elicit the sub modalities of food you hate

Now think of a food that you do not like at all. Imagine eating it as you smell and taste it, how it makes you feel. Are you sick? Probably so, now take note of all the sub modalities involved in disliking this food. Imagine what you would feel like chewing and swallowing the food.

Step Three: The difference between the like and disliked food

There are some definite differences here as there should be. One food you like and the other you despise. The differences in the two are called drivers. The steak is hot and smells good. Deviled eggs are cold and smell nasty. Steak is dark and pleasing to the eye while the deviled eggs are different colors with a much different texture.

Step Four: Replacing the likes with dislikes

Now imagine that hot and juicy steak, but replace it with those deviled eggs. Imagine yourself eating those deviled eggs, how they taste and what they feel like going down. Imagine that steak tastes like those eggs that you absolutely hate. Separate yourself from that steak by stepping out and making the visual smaller. How bad do you want that steak now?

Step Five: Test it

This replacement method is a great way to neutralize those cravings. This method can help individuals turn off those cravings and callings for things that they do not need or are bad for them. Granted, you would not always want to replace and never eat steak again, but this can be used as a tool to control the intensity and state of mind.

Magic Information Gathering

What do you want?

What would that do for you?

How will you know when you have it?

(What will you see, hear or feel that is your evidence you have this?)

What's important to you about that?

What's important to you about that?

Values – Your Driving Force

Have you ever heard someone say that people are driven by emotions rather than logic, and that is their downfall? People do take action based on the way that they feel, because they are human. A one hundred percent logical creature would act more like a robot with a lack of emotion or empathy for others. This being said, emotions and feelings are sometimes the restricting vice for many. It can be fear, lack of motivation or any number of other reasons, but never the less it is an emotional fear instead of a logical one.

Most people understand that a habit such as over eating or smoking can cause them great harm. The habit is costly, frowned upon and can cause serious health concerns, yet emotionally the individual continues the habit as a form of control. Logically, they tell themselves that continuing the habit will harm them, but there is an emotional payoff from the feeling that the habit provides. A sense of control, calming, good feeling or any other positive feeling is the payout that the individual feels.

The emotions being referred to can fall into two categories; negative or positive. Individuals are driven to move toward a positive emotion and as far away from negative emotions as possible. As humans we enjoy feeling good, positive feedback and responses that leave us smiling at the end of the day. These positive emotions give people feelings of security, power and often a high level of confidence. On the other hand negative emotions can promote fear, insecurity, depression and lack of or low confidence levels.

An Amoeba – A What

Do you remember watching amoebas in junior high science class? Under the magnifying glass you could see these tiny organisms move between negative and positive emotions. They would move toward food and certainly away from a source of heat. People are the exact same way, well a few differences, but the same theory. We move toward success, freedom and happiness, leaving rejection or embarrassment behind.

Think about situations such as marriage. People long for a life of happiness and companionship, no one wants to be by themselves or lonely. Think about how hard most people try to find a positive relationship and get married. It is because they have attached marriage and union to positive emotions, away from negative emotions. Some people on the other hand view marriage as a loss of freedom and reason to bicker. These individuals have attached a very different emotion to the issue of marriage, therefore wishing to avoid it.

Everyone wants to achieve positive emotions that lead to happiness, security and a good life. Though people attach different emotions to different situations the desire for positive feelings and situations is the same.

Moving Toward Values

A person may differ in their attachment of values to situations. For example, some people view marriage as a union of happiness, while others view it as a loss of freedom. These are the differences in values and how the person is drawn to positive emotions. This theory can be seen clearly by viewing different people. Two people that have different emotions to situations will typically live very different lives. This is because their theories and where they are drawn are very different. Take for example an individual that is deeply drawn to security and consistency. He would be most likely to avoid risky behavior, be a spend thrift or have a flashy job that is not secure. This individual would live very differently from someone that attached positive emotions to excitement, change and loved to spend money. The two would likely take different vacations, spend differently and spend their time much differently.

Having a good understanding of your personal values and driving emotions can help stay focused. Significant emotions are move towards goals that determine values. It is highly important to develop values that enable one to move toward positive emotions and stay away from negative ones.

How Values Drive Behavior

Understanding that significant emotions drive values can help explain the success or lack thereof in your life. After discovering values and what you are moving toward or away from gives a good indication of where you are going in life. Many people do not have clear cut goals in life leading to indecisiveness and leading them to lose their passion. After coming to this understanding of values it is easy to see the problem with achieving goals and succeeding. It is hard to change what you do not know, this way you can determine and move toward positives.

Values Definition

Values can be defined very differently by people. What is successful for one may not matter to another even though the value may be the same. Many people claim to value success, but what is success. Well, it depends on the individual and what emotional significance they hold in reference to success. For one success may be making millions every year and for another it may be saving a life. No two people are the same, values are defined by the person. Those with similar values will often work very differently to achieve them. This is because they are working for what is important or the positive emotions that have been placed on the value.

Mother Theresa and Madonna both longed to touch the lives of people and have great success in doing so. While most people would argue that the two were nowhere on the same level, they both aspired to be successful. For Madonna the help for mankind was singing music, lifting the spirit. Mother Theresa on the other hand sought to feed the hungry and bring comfort through spirituality. No the same roads were not taken and the path was far from the same, but the value of success was the same.

Analyzing Your Values

To truly understand how you have become what you are, you must understand the values that you are moving toward as well as what you are moving away from. These away values are as important to understand as the toward values, because it gives you guidance. Granted you must understand the path to the goals, but you also must know what to stay away from!

Understanding your inner self can be obtained by making a list of toward values and away from values. Rating these can help determine the issues and problems that may have been holding you back from success. If a goal has been achieved, you may want to make a note about how you achieved it and why. This can give you guidance to achieving another!

Emotionally Charge Values

Neural patterns were formed by emotional experiences that developed associations for values. This is a pattern that is conditioned in the nervous experience and to associate a new value it takes following this pattern. The pattern involves repetition of the emotion using visualization and the changing of sub modalities. Visualization is a highly important part of associating an emotion with a value. Just like learning anything else it is important to rehearse and burn this theory into the mind. By visualizing the goal, you can set yourself up for success. Envisioning yourself in the place of succeeding with the goal, will help you maintain focus. This focus gives you the confidence and energy to continue on the path to success.

New Values – New Life

After determining a new value, it is important to take steps toward the goal. Make a plan, map it out and then follow through. This may mean making new choices, changing habits and certainly living a little different. Through rehearsal and envisioning yourself in that success light, you will find the positive image to continue on.

If you run into negativity or rejection along the way, do not take it as a negative. Reframe the experience and learn from the feedback. This feedback can provide the needed experience to make it through and achieve.

How to Get Your Goals Using Your Brain?

Everyone wants to succeed and be the best that they can be, so what is holding most people back? Many people speak a good game and they understand that they must have goals and dreams to achieve the money, freedom and great lifestyle that they desire. But, when it actually comes to planning and having the correct goals, people often fail miserably. For most, their goal consists of only the things that they desire, not true long lasting goals. Now many would say what is the problem with that? It is simple, when your goals are only driven by immediate or short-term desires, you will be left feeling frustrated and disappointed when they are not achieved. The key is looking to personality changes and behavioral changes when looking to goals. If you change the way that you think about your goals, you will succeed. But, if you are only looking for that $100,000 car, you may be disappointed.

When individuals set goals they must reach for the stars, (which is the easy part) and then be truly committed to what they desire. FOCUSED ATTENTION IS VITAL! If you get frustrated because success does not fall in your lap, you will spend the rest of your days agitated and never get anything productive accomplished. Think about it this way, if you really want something, you know that you have to continue working until you achieve it. Take this example, if a person wants to succeed in business, yet is not willing to make the necessary contacts, give countless hours and work hard, how far do you think he/she will get? The answer is not very far. To achieve goals individuals, have to be able to think outside the box and be willing to work for it and change their thinking. You must be willing to step outside your comfort level and push ahead. Failure is not an option.

Setting Yourself Up for Success

Have you ever heard of the extraordinary power or strength of a mother whose child was in danger? Do you know why she was able to achieve that "goal" of protecting her child? It is because, when people's goals are a necessity they're thinking changes. The excuses and procrastination becomes a pushing force to cause them to act toward their goal. When people are required to achieve their goals they stand up to the pressure and go the extra mile to ensure that the actions get complete. This is because there is a sense of urgency and need. This is an excellent quality in the human mind, because what it allows us to see is the fact that we can control our motivation and programming of functions.

It is all in your "self-talk" and the words that you feed to yourself every day. You must set yourself up for success. The excuses and "will do tomorrows" have to cease and there needs to be a sense of urgency in completing your goal. Do you think if a person told you that if you didn't lose the weight, put down the cigarettes or booze that he was going to kill your loved one, that you wouldn't stop that behavior? You bet, because the stakes are raised and you are requiring more of yourself. You are also giving yourself positive feedback in the fact that you are telling yourself you must achieve, or else.

There are very few individuals in this world that are incapable of achieving their goals and success in their lives. When it becomes a "must" to succeed people pull all the stops and jump all the hurdles in life. The best way to accomplish this is to raise the stakes and give yourself the credit that you deserve. Do not sell yourself short, this is why people fail. They give themselves negative feedback and give up because they feel that they just simply cannot meet the expectations of the goal. This is where the frustration comes in and they eventually give up and look for a new goal to have. Instead of a "should" your goal has to become a "must", if it doesn't you are in fear of failing.

Think About Your Past Achievements

Think back to the events in your life and your past goals. What was your mindset, why was it achieved and did you give up along the way? The chances are that there was a point and time that you thought about throwing in the towel, but didn't. For some reason your goal was "a must" to you, it may have been a job, money or other reason, but you achieved it. Take this example and draw from the behavior. When it comes time to file your taxes, did you get it done? The answer is yes, because you knew if you didn't that you would have to answer to the taxman. (A subject I truly know) Think about that education, you knew if you did not finish, you would spend the rest of your days making minimum wage or worse digging a ditch. It was a requirement (must) and you knew that no matter what the obstacle you must overcome it. It is no different with the goals that you set in life, you must tell yourself that you have no choice. There is no room for quitting or tomorrow, it must be done today.

Take a few minutes and think of the things that you want to accomplish, but have been putting off. Be honest with yourself and give no slack. Do not start making excuses, that is the reason you have not succeeded today. List these 3 things and then we will look at how to get the ball rolling.

1.

2.

3.

Raise The Bar On Your Acceptance Level

When we dream we generally dream big, like owning a high dollar home or car, but when we set our goals we settle. Sure we would like to make $10,000 a month, but we are willing to settle for $3000 per month. Why is this? We sell ourselves short, every time. If we settle, then we do not reach for any other expectations and will be left settling for the rest of our lives. If we are satisfied with $3000 per month, but continue on to achieve the $10,000 per month and continue working, we will achieve the higher amount. People gravitate to their goals, especially when they feel that they must. Think about it this way, when you are short on cash for the month, but the bills haven't been paid and the cabinets are bare, you pull some over time. You know that you must achieve another $500 dollars or your family will have no electricity and be hungry, which is not acceptable or an option. So regardless of how tired you are or worn out you continue on to achieve that goal. That is because you have raised your expectation level and are telling yourself you cannot settle for what you have today.

Change Your Language

Give up words such as should, would, could and if. They can no longer be a part of your goal or dreams. Instead of "I wish" it becomes "I will", it may sound trivial or silly, but it truly works. Listen to individuals that have obtained great success in their lives. Look at people like Donald Trump, Bill Clinton and others that have achieved the ultimate success in their lives. Do you hear their speech, is it I wished I could of? NO! They speak as if everything is a work in progress that is because it is. They continually reach for higher standards and dreams. They do not settle because they sell themselves short.

You must foster your creativity, be good to yourself and allow yourself to grow. If you do not grow as a person, your dreams and goals will go right out the window. A positive self-esteem and identity is one of the most important feats in achieving success. So, instead of telling yourself that you will do that tomorrow, tell yourself it will be completed today. No more settling for excuses of why you can't achieve a goal. There is no choice and it has become a must, because could of, would of and should of are gone from our vocabulary.

You have to start using must language with your internal dialog. You will respond more to those things that you "MUST" do, so if you raise the bar on your inner dialog, it will bring it to new levels. I also suggest you adopt the phrase in your big goals, "Failure is not an option". Remember when Cortez landed in the New World, he burned the boats, so his men knew that they could not fail, try these inner attitudes on for a change!

Bibliography

Cialdini Ph. D., Robert B.. Influence: The Psychology of Persuasion (Collins Business Essentials) (p. 46). Harper-Collins. Kindle Edition.

Greene, Robert. The 48 Laws Of Power (The Robert Greene Collection) (Kindle Location 9025). Profile Books. Kindle Edition

Hogan, Kevin. (1996). *Psychology of Persuasion* [E -Reader Version].

Hogan, Kevin and Horton, William D. (2002). *Selling Yourself to Others, The New Psychology* of Sales [E -Reader Version].

Horton, William D. (2014). *Advanced Secret Mind Control* [E -Reader Version].

Horton, William D. (2015). Primary Objective, Neuro Linguistic Psychology and Guerilla Warfare [E -Reader Version].

Horton, William D. (2013). *Quantum Psychology* [E -Reader Version].

Bibliography Cont'd

Horton, William D. (2013). *Secret Mind Control* [E -Reader Version].

Horton, William D. (2013). *The Alcohol and Addiction Solution* [E -Reader Version].

"Marxist Dreams and Soviet Realities," Marxist Dreams and Soviet Realities, AU: Mises Institute.

Raaflaub, Kurt A.; Ober, Josiah; Wallace, Robert, eds. (2007). Origins of Democracy in Ancient Greece. Berkeley: University of California Press.

The enemy of my enemy is my friend - Wikipedia. (ND). Retrieved from https://en.wikipedia.org/wiki/The_enemy_of_my_enemy_is_my_friend

The One-Sentence Persuasion Course - Action Plan... (ND). Retrieved from http://www.actionplan.com/pdf/BlairWarren.pdf

Treaty of Versailles/Preamble, retrieved in 2016 from https://en.wikisource.org/wiki/Treaty_of_Versailles/Preamble

Made in the USA
Middletown, DE
21 September 2019